ORIGINAL MONOLOGUES FOR WOMEN

by Robes Kossez

SAMUEL FRENCH, INC.
45 West 25th Street NEW YORK 10010
7623 Sunset Boulevard HOLLYWOOD 90046
LONDON TORONTO

IMPORTANT BILLING AND CREDIT REQUIREMENTS

All producers of ORIGINAL MONOLOGUES FOR WOMEN *must* give credit to the Author of the monologue in all programs distributed in connection with performances of the monologue and in all instances in which the title of the monologue appears for purposes of advertising, publicizing or otherwise exploiting the monologue and/or a production. The name of the Author *must* also appear on a separate line, on which no other name appears, immediately following the title, and *must* appear in size of type not less than fifty percent the size of the title type.

ISBN 0 573 60115 1 Printed in U.S.A.

PREFACE

Why did I write this monologue book?

I have been a professional actor since my early teens, and only after many years of performing did I begin to write plays. Having been on both sides of the footlights, I began to think, who is more qualified to write for actors than a playwright who has been an actor?

I know what you want. A monologue that is not a speech, but rather a character you can make your own, that will reveal your special talents, and make your audience sit up and take notice. And do you know what I want as a playwright, as I listen to auditions all day long? An actor who will make me sit up and take notice.

CONTENTS

A FIRST-TIME JOGGER RUNS AFTER ROMANCE

Comic

Why am I doing this? I know why I'm doing this. Because this outfit and my shoes set me back a couple of hundred. Just once around the track, if I make it, then I call it quits. (*SHE looks to her side.*) Well, hello. *(SHE smiles.*) You do? Oh, I'm so glad you like my form. I do this all the time. Five times a week in rain or snow. And by your form, it looks as if you do this all the time, too. Would you mind running a little slower? Just want to shake myself out. Who do you work for? Oh, you don't work for anyone—everyone works for you? Isn't that nice. I mean, that's really nice. I like bossy men. I mean, men who are their own bosses. They usually make all the money. Oh, no kidding. I know people who've bought co-ops, but I've never known anyone who bought the entire building. In what part of the twenty-two floors do you live? I knew you would say that. I didn't have to ask. The top part, of course. Would you mind running a little slower? Dare I ask who with? You know, the top part. Who lives with you in the top part? A Weimaraner. Oh, two Weimaraners. Isn't that cozy. Any people? I mean, do any people inhabit the top part of the twenty-two floors? No people. Just servants. Oh, isn't that nice. I mean that's really nice. How neat. Just two Weimaraners and ten servants running all around the top half of a twenty-two floor building. Would you mind running a little slower? I don't mind running after you, but you really are running too fast. Now tell me. I'm dying to know. Do you ever have any people staying overnight in the top half of your twenty-two floor building? You do? What? Your buddies. Oh, hell, that does it. I'm stopping to tie my shoe. (*SHE bends down ready to collapse from exhaustion.)* Why are you running around me? Why are you running in circles around me? Because you like me. I'm a girl. You've noticed. How much have you noticed? Oh, that much. Really. How nice of you to say so. If you want to run circles around me, be my guest, but I do have to find out a few things. Why don't you have any girls running around the top half of your twenty-two story building? Because you're shy? No kidding. Then why aren't you shy with me? Because I remind you of your mother. And your sister. And your cousin, who had a mad crush on you but couldn't marry you because the blood in your family is too thin. How old are you? That young, that handsome, that rich and in such good form—not to mention my blood is thick. Come on, let's run. If I die of a heart attack it will be worth it. *(SHE begins to run again.)* Would you mind running a little slower? What? Why, no. I'm not doing anything at all for the rest of my life, so pick the night. Why are you running faster? Because I've stimulated your glands? Please run slower, you're getting ahead of me. What? When? What's your name? Damn it! Come back here. I can't hear you! *(SHE slowly stops running.)* Oh, shit! Just when I had him, he ran away.

A TALK WITH DAD, AFTER THE FUNERAL

Serious

I never saw you cry, Dad, until today. I thought you would break down at the hospital, but you didn't. I even watched you at the funeral parlor. Nothing. And when they lowered Mom down into that big hole, to rot, not a tear. Oh, come on, Dad, that's what's going to happen. Mom's beginning to rot already. I don't think it's an ugly thought. That's only Mom's poor tired body that's rotting. Her spirit is here, right in this house. She's listening to us and laughing. No wonder you cried when you came home. You must have heard her whisper something to you and you mistook her whisper for a memory. Seeing you cry made me feel good. You have always been so strong and there was never a moment in my life when I thought I couldn't come to you and you would make it all better. Your approval—wheee!—meant everything. And you gave it so willingly. It's as if the Almighty came down and patted me on the head. When you disapproved, which was seldom, that's when a brick wall would go up in front of me and I knew I couldn't fight it. I know you loved Mom but did you have good sex with her? No, no, no. This *is* the time to ask these questions. When all our senses have been violated—now is the time for confessions and good stuff like that. I've never had good sex, Dad. Oh, the anticipation of it drives me wild but the actual act is nothing. And I'm in my early twenties, yet I know I won't get married. You should have had more than one kid because you will never have any grandchildren. Is that sad? Does that hurt you? I want to know because after tonight, you will never tell me. Tonight is a tender night. I can almost see your guts through your skin. Do you want to get married again? Would you marry someone like Mom or someone different? Don't stay alone. I love you, but I won't be here, Dad, when you get old, to take care of you. Tonight I feel as if I can look straight into the future. I hurt all over because I know I won't have Mom to come home to anymore. Is that why I feel so alive? No. No. I can't stop it, Dad. I can't. It's raw nerve time. Tomorrow our skins will harden and protect us. And by next year, we will be back again, as we always were. Why did I like you more than Mom? Oh, I feel so guilty that she died first. It would have been easier if you were the one, rotting in the grave. No. No. I won't be quiet. That way, Mom and I would be close and we would only talk about you. And I hate to tell you this because I'm going to destroy your only dream. Boom! I'm not going to make it through medical school. Come on, Dad, let's face it together. I'm above average but I'm not that smart. In any case, I can't be what you want. It's been your dream and now the dream is over. Tell me how it feels for it to be over—Boom! Like that. And now that Mom is dead—dead as a doornail. Dead—I will love you more, but your approval, or disapproval, will mean less. And no matter how much we want her back, we will never hear her laughter at the dinner table. So—let the rage surge in you—and cry. That's right, Dad. Let the rage tear us apart—and cry.

A YOUNG GIRL THINKS SHE NEEDS A SHRINK

Comic

Do you think I need a shrink? I mean, I'm a little crazy. Like—I hate my mom. Sometimes I could kill her. Oh, but I mean if something ever happened to her I think I would die. Just die. I hate my boyfriend, too. I don't mean like hate. I mean like HATE! No, not Jack, I don't even like Jack so how can I hate him? Bummer. He's such a joke, you know. You know what I mean. Last night he was just all over me, and I do mean all over. ALL over. That really sucks. I hate him so much that tonight I'm going to see him again. So I can get rid of all this hate I have for him. Maybe he'll start to hate me and then I could maybe start to feel something for him and want him to paw me all over. And I do mean all over. I think that's sick. Don't you think that's sick? And another thing. I don't know what to do with my life. I don't know whether I really want to be a movie star. Or a physicist. Or go to bed with my history teacher, Mr. Berlinger. Of course, all I think about is going to bed with my history teacher, Mr. Berlinger. And he's so old, too. Of course he's old. He has a two-year-old kid, doesn't he, and he's married and has his Masters. I mean, that's what I call old and experienced. That's all I think about is his experience—in bed. That's sick. I mean that's really sick to be hung up on an old man. And another thing—and I hate to tell you this, but I've got to tell someone, or I'll just die. I cheated on my algebra test. How else could I get a B plus? And if I cheated on an algebra test at my age, can you imagine what kind of cheating I'll do when I graduate? I'm depraved. I know I'm depraved and I think that's sick. So that's why I think I'm going to see this shrink. That's all I think about. Going to see him week after week, telling him all about my depraved sexual fantasies. And oh, Ginnie, he's so cute! Can you imagine seeing him week after week, having an orgasm every time I do? Now, don't you think that's sick? I think that's sick. Like—yuck! That's why I've just got to see this shrink! Or I think I'll go crazy.

HARD, TOUGH AND WORLDLY

Serio-comic

So I'll die in my glorious prime instead of at eighty, when I'll be riddled with arthritis and won't know what the hell my name is. Like Grandma up there. Jesus, when you drink scotch neat and have a few belts everyone thinks you're stinko. It's those sweet young things who sip their fruit punches through pinky straws who get stinko. Closet drunks. Sweety drunks. Sloppy drunks. I hold my liquor like Dad. Except I didn't inherit his kindness. If you want to know the truth, I've become as ruthless as hell. So, Doc, what do you think of your sis after all these years? Tabby is what you used to call me, never thinking I'd one day become a hellcat. I wish she would die and get it over with so we can leave with all her dirty old money. In fact, Doc, I think you should give me your share. What do you need it for? Good practice, devoted wife, and wonderful children. Five! I knew Sally was a rabbit the minute I saw her. It was the way she chewed her lettuce—like this. Sweet, sweet Sally, gave you five paunchy brats and I bet she's lousy in the sack. My poor brother. You really did deserve better. But so did I. Married a queer—well, he might as well have been. Got it up at Christmas, New Year's and Flag Day. Damn! He was a real humper before I married him. What a specimen. It's stupid to castrate what you want. Then—married a talented, sensitive man who turned out to be a lousy cheat. Cheated me out of all my money—then split. Why does she want to live? It's over, Grandma! Do you hear me? She does, you know. It gives her satisfaction to keep me waiting. I don't blame her. I would do the same. They kicked me off the school board because a little tomcat told on Tabby. That's why I started to write those dirty books. They don't pay as much as you think, so you should really give me your share. Shouldn't he, Grandma? She's over eighty, God damn her! You'd think she'd be tired of living. But no—she lives on. It's you who's tired of living, Doc, and you have five children instead of none, and you have patients you would love to kill, and you can't get out and ride a horse anymore, knowing that your dream of becoming a cowboy was as fake as those movies you used to love. You're trapped and you're tired of living and, God damn it, I don't want to see it. We were great kids, though. We had good, solid, no-nonsense parents and we all lived the good life. Cherry pie with vanilla ice cream on top, every Saturday, can't be all that bad. Mom and Dad had the decency to die when they should. So hurry up, Grandma. You're past your time. She always took my part in everything. Spoiled me rotten, as she did you. Made me feel as if I were special. That's why I want her to die. Quick, let's get it over, Grandma! Tonight she looked at me with those blue ashen eyes, still clear enough to see what I've become. No incriminations. No judgments. Just love. That's why you've got to die tonight, because I don't want to see myself reflected in your eyes! I should have stayed away, but you see I really do need the money, and I thought I could convince you to give me yours. You're a good man, brother. And me—the hellcat who became an alley cat—I'm rotten. But Grandma thinks I'm good, and as long as she's alive—shhh. I can feel it in my chest. A heart just stopped beating. A beautiful heart. Shit. I wish it were mine.

WEDDING RINGS HAVE TO BE SOLD

Serious

Oh, what a beautiful morning, isn't it? Now, let me see, they're right in here. I wrapped them in tissue paper. There! A wedding band and an engagement ring. Aren't they beautiful? They're my mother's. She never wears them much anymore. Dad died ten years ago and she's frightened of losing them. New? What do you mean, new? How can you tell a new diamond from an old one? Oh, you mean the settings look new. I can see you're an expert. They are. Around five years old. Silly, isn't it, my pretending they're my mother's. I mean, why should you care who they belong to, you're only interested in the diamonds. You see—they're mine, as a matter of fact. I don't know why I didn't tell you that in the first place. I have some debts and need the money. I hate to part with them. My husband died a year ago and I need the money to pay some bills. You know how they pile up—so—I thought I would sell—these. I think you will find they are excellent diamonds. I'm afraid Jim spoiled me. Nothing was too much for me then. I—remember when he bought me my engagement ring. It was—I think I'd better not talk about it. Oh, no. No. I do want to sell them. As I said, I need the money. I don't need the money and you know it. I see that you are looking at my pearls and, I can tell you know they are very expensive. You see—Jim gave me the pearls on our first anniversary. But, of course, that doesn't concern you, now does it? You're only interested in the quality of the stones. And they are good, aren't they? Jim was always a generous man. As I said, he gave me everything I wanted. As a matter of fact, he still does. Guilt, I suppose. Why he has to be guilty, I really don't know. It wasn't totally his fault, yet, I still can't understand—(*SHE laughs.*) Do you know, this is worse than seeing a psychiatrist for the first time. As you can gather, my husband is not dead. In fact, he's very much alive. I don't know why I'm making up all these lies. It's really very foolish of me.

Why should you care if the rings are mine and that I don't need the money? Or if my husband is dead or alive? Or if I divorced him, or if he divorced me? Or even if we were happy—which we were. I know you're only interested in making some money. But—I can't tell you how terrible it is for me to see you handle my rings in such a dispassionate way, calculating how much they are worth. And really—what are they worth? You can't tell me. Five years I wore them and I have such sweet memories of what we shared with each other. I designed the wedding band myself. Jim was so proud of me. He had the jeweler copy my plans exactly. He kept bringing them back, telling him it wasn't right. The poor man sighed with relief when it was all over. And the engagement ring, did you notice the setting? We argued about that for days. Jim was frightened that it was too fragile and that someday I would lose the stone. Well, he was right about that, wasn't he—in a way. Oh, yes, I'm quite certain I want to sell them. You see—I can't—bear—to look at them anymore. So, what is it going to be? I want a good price. How much are they worth?

A YOUNG GIRL, THE LAST TENANT

Serious

Do you suppose it will snow, today, old man? If it does, I know you will tell me. It must be after three. I can hear the children coming home from school. You can tell time by children. How many years have you been the super in this old building, old man? (*SHE laughs.*) I wasn't even born then. Listen—how quiet this building has become. Downstairs on the first floor, there's a loose board that creaks when you walk by. And on the fourth, the doors rattle. I miss the people. Just the two of us now. How sad, old man. Soon your Lady House will be coming down. Now, don't start. I don't care how many times my aunt has called, I'm not going to live with her. No, old man, I don't have to! (*SHE begins to mold a figure in clay.*) Do you know what one critic said about my sculpture? He said I was searching for my soul with the hope that I wouldn't find it. Don't say that! The end is not coming! I'm going to find a new place, that's all. And I'm going to do the things I want. With my hands I'm going to mold in clay all the things I know—like the cold and heat of the city. The sounds buses make, the hissing of radiators on cold afternoons, and all the cats I've ever known. I'm going to make them tall, straight and independent. And yet, old man—sometimes after I wash the dishes and put them away, that's when I begin to listen to the sounds of the city, the sounds that tell me it's night. There's usually a fire engine screeching to somewhere, and often a police siren in the distance. But last night I heard a scream from somewhere. No, it wasn't really a scream. It was more like a low, deep whimper for help. The city became so quiet after that. I lay back in the silence and felt, if only I could reach out into the darkness and comfort this unknown pain. Don't you see? I don't want to be taken care of. I don't want to feel useless. I want to feel important. I want to feel needed. It's just sometimes I feel lost. (*Pause.*) Oh, has it? Has it really started to snow, old man? Is it coming down in large flakes? Is it? If only I could see it.

A CONNECTICUT HOUSEWIFE GOES TO A SOHO PARTY

Comic

My—isn't this chic? Isn't this quaint? Isn't this avant-garde? A party in a dirty old loft. You see—I come from Connecticut where there's nothing like this. This is a breath of fresh air. Rye and ginger, please. My, what a spread. I just love it—love it—love it. Just look at this table. Everything doesn't match. All the magazines say nothing should match these days. Now in Connecticut everyone's trying not to match. But, you see, I was born in Queens where everything matches, so I'm having a hard time. Oh—you don't know what Connecticut is like. Children and children and chitter, chatter. And car pools. Kids, kids, kids all over the place. And barbecues. They're so depressing. Grass—grass—grass. Weed—weed—weed to make it grow. And then you have to cut—cut—cut. It's so senseless. PTA and cookie sales. And dreary nights around the fireplace. One night, I almost threw myself in. I had a few rye and gingers and had this violent urge to throw myself into the fireplace. I kicked over my sweet little mosaic coffee table and the room was in a shambles. (*SHE turns.*) My, you're an artist, aren't you? I just knew you were an artist the minute I came in because of your beard. I just love disheveled men with beards. Now tell—tell—tell. Tell me all about your beautiful and tragic life. Now, don't you get discouraged, no matter what terrible things people say about your paintings. Just look at van Gogh. Suffered—suffered—suffered. Then he died and look what happened. He became rich and famous. Maybe you can help me. I have this enormous wall at home that I don't know what to do with. Maybe you have an enormous canvas. Something you're dying to get rid of—cheap. I'm looking for something blue and orange to match my slipcovers. I prefer sweet little oceansides with sweet little people running after each other. In blue and orange. Now, if you have something that's not too abstract, I'd like to look at it. I hate paintings that are too abstract. They get me so depressed. Once I was looking at this painting. And then suddenly I saw all these dirty things in it. All these people running after each other, doing these dirty things. I must have looked at that painting for an hour. Now I wouldn't want anything like that to cover up my big white wall. Oh, it must be wonderful to be an artist. I mean to be moody and suffer and have tragic love affairs with married ladies. I know, why don't you paint me? Frolicking at the oceanside with someone frolicking after me. Naked, perhaps? Naked is not dirty. I know; I'm a liberal.

AFTER TWENTY-ONE YEARS, MARRIAGE IS A BORE

Comic

Oh, Bob, what are you doing here? We may not have a legal separation but we do have a private one. Who cares if everyone knows? After twenty-one years you should be bored with me. I'm bored with you. I mean, it's only natural. After being married for twenty-one years, we both should be bored with each other. And if you're not bored with me, then there must be something unnatural about you. And if you're still in love with me, then you must be sick. After twenty-one years it's positively freakish for you to be in love with me. Ick! It makes my skin crawl. I'm the only wife I know, who is sorry her husband never cheated on her. If you did, you would have someone to keep you company by now and you wouldn't be bothering me. The problem with you, my darling, is that you're in a rut. I know we've both been in a rut for the past twenty-one years, but now you're in a rut all by yourself. I suppose we've had our good times, but we've never had any deliriously wonderful times. Of course I know that's not what marriage is about. Why in hell do you think I want a divorce? Now, let me tell you what I think you should do. I think you should pick up someone and have an affair. I'm quite sure there are many foolish young girls out there who will think you're interesting. And they may even delude themselves into thinking you're sexy. So, go. Get out of my life and live in a bar. That's where all these desperate young girls are. And don't worry, they're not choosy. They'll think you're wonderful, until they get to know you. What do you mean you don't know how to pick up a girl? Then learn! You will? You can't wait? It sounds like fun? Go, Bob. And if you're not back for dinner—then—I'll—I'll—keep it warm. *(SHE cries.)*

A YOUNG SCIENTIST DECIDES TO FALL IN LOVE

Comic

Hi, sis. I bought pasta, tomatoes and ricotta cheese. I'm through with seaweed, yogurt and alfalfa sprouts. I've decided to do something desperate, something that will change my life. Cook. What does it matter if I'm brilliant? Just because I'm a genius it doesn't mean I can't cook. I think Einstein did. I want to eat cholesterol, drink wine and damage some of my brain cells. And if I try hard enough, I'm sure I can be as foolish and commonplace as anyone else. Why? So I can have some fun. I know I never wanted to have any fun, but I do now. I want to be sophisticated and sexy like you. And a little dumb. I'm tired of dissecting mice all day. I'm tired of writing brilliant reports at night. The men I know are only interested in one thing—stealing my ideas! None of them would dream of taking advantage of me. Well I'm sick of it! I want to he taken advantage of. I know I've never been interested in boys. Who cares if I never went out on a date? Even though I don't know much about men, I can learn. I'm quite sure there's not that much to find out. I know you've always thought of me as a rare mutation—but why can't a rare mutation flirt like a dizzy blonde? Don't you see, sis, my life is a closed book and no man has ever wanted to open it. And if they tried, I made sure there was too much written there so they would never have room to doodle. Well, I've changed. I'm going to make myself a blank page and let them doodle as much as they want. I know I never cared that much about sex. I just underrated it, that's all. Get the door, sis. It's a homo sapiens masculus coming into conjunction with a homo sapiens femina over dinner. And I did cook dinner. I never thought it would be so easy. All you have to do is put it all in one pot and let it simmer, and then go to a long movie. Sis, to think, tonight I'm finally going to be written upon. Quick, get the door. (*SHE fluffs up her hair and unbuttons a button on her blouse.*) Wait.

Look at me. I don't look too smart, do I? What is there to be worried about? I was always a whiz at biology.

A BEGGAR TELLS A COFFEE-SHOP OWNER ABOUT HER DAY

Comic

I'm not a bum! How many times do I have to tell ya that. I'm a beggar! There's a difference. Everywhere you go you see the bums. Don't mistake them for us. We beggars are a dying race. Thank you, Mr. Hill, for the hot tea. Now, if it isn't too much trouble, would ya put a little honey in it? I don't even ask ya for some cream, but a dried up jelly roll would do just fine. You know, Mr. Hill, I don't know where to put my head down anymore. The subways are not what they used to be. (*SHE drinks.*) Hmmmm, this hits the spot. But it could be sweeter. It was cold in St. Mark's Place today. Suddenly the wind came up like fury as if out of nowhere. It whipped up the leaves and blew soot in people's eyes. When it's cold and it looks like snow, that's when I get the most money. A man gave me a quarter, and a lady with white hair gave me a nickle. Imagine that! A nickle! That's the old biddies for ya. Some college boys came by—they never give you anything. A woman with a tiny dog took out a half-dollar and I think she said, thank you. You can always rely on people with dogs. A little more hot water wouldn't be bad, and if ya have another old tea bag someone left behind, you could put that in too. Hmmmm, this jelly roll is good, but it's as hard as a brick. The monkey didn't come by today—my competition. But that lousy well-dressed man, who thinks he's such a hot shot, did. He was ready to pass me as always, acting as if I wasn't even there. But then, something made him stop. I knew someday I would get him. He dug deep into his pocket and with two beautifully manicured nails, he plucked out a fiver and gave it to me. I'll tell ya, there's a lot of fools in this world today. You bet your life. And then, some kids came by and gave me pennies. Why shouldn't I take money from children? It teaches them how to give. And that, Mr. Hill, is the difference between the bums and the beggars. There's a need for us in the world, even though the bums are taking over, and we're a dying race.

SISTERLY LOVE

Serious

Do you remember what you once told me, Ted? It was a long time ago when we were children. We were out on the back porch, looking up at the moon. It was a night very much like this, and you said that if you lie in the light of the moon, the moon will purify. If you stretch yourself out in the light of the moon—the moon will bleach out the sin that is in you. And I reached out my hands to the moon, closed my eyes and let the moonlight bathe over me, because I believed you. Mama was somewhere in the house, but we were old enough to know. You should have let me go, but you wouldn't. I think Mama would have let me go if it hadn't been for you. You took everything out of my suitcase and put it all neatly back in my drawer. Then Dad and Mama sided with you, and I never did go. And then at dinner we all sat around the table and it wasn't even mentioned. Dad told me never to speak of it again and I never did. I do what everyone tells me. I say what they want me to say. It's because I don't want to hurt anybody. It's a great failing. I love Him! No, I won't stop it now. I love Him! I love God! It's the only thing I ever really wanted. But you said no, then Mama and Dad said no, so it didn't happen. I never told Sister Agatha my secret. I tried, but I couldn't. "And why do you want to become a nun?" she used to say. "Guilt, Sister." I never told her. Peace and the need to forget. But most important, to have God's salvation, for Him to give me the courage to rid myself of the terrible thing I had within me. I loved Sister Agatha so much. She made me feel beautiful and clean inside. And during those few hours I spent with her, life seemed simple—for those few moments, I was at peace and truly happy. Piece by piece you took the things out of my bag and I never spoke of it. We all had dinner. It was the only thing I ever wanted, and no one mentioned it. I did the dishes, you went off to the movies, Mama went inside to read the paper, and Dad looked at me for just a moment—as if he knew.

And then went out on the back porch with his book. And that was the end. You owe me something, Teddy, because of that ! Oh, yes, you do! You owe me! I want you to promise that you will never tell Dad or Mama or anybody—about us.

A WOMAN IN LOVE, WITHOUT A MIND OF HER OWN

Comic

You really are despicable, Jim. It took me a long time to find out what kind of bastard you are. You can't do this! It's unfair! How cruel! I refuse to allow you to divorce your wife because of me! Oh, don't give me that. You love her, I know you do. In fact, you can't get along without her. If you divorce her, who do you think is going to pick out your neckties? Me? Forget it! Who's going to take your clothes to the cleaners? I can barely do that for myself. And who is going to cook? Why do you think we love each other so much—we eat in restaurants. Now, you know I adore you. I'm mad for you. I would be lost without you. But that's no reason why you have to divorce your wife and marry me. You really know how to hurt a woman. You see, my darling, it just wouldn't work. I know myself. I am in touch with what I want from a man. I've been through therapy twice. If we got married, you would only end up divorcing me, and since you're happily married now what's the point? Let's face it, a little of me goes a long way, and too much of me can make you sick. Oh, yes, I've made a lot of men sick. I'm all strawberries and whipped cream, without the biscuit. And without the biscuit there's no strawberry shortcake. And that's what marriage is all about. Oh, so what if your wife's just a biscuit. Little biscuits can be fun. Not wild fun, but fun. You can't deny she's always made you feel comfortable and content. What have I ever done for you, but to work you up into a wild passionate animal and given you unending pleasure? Suddenly I'm beginning to convince myself that I should marry you. No! I must be strong, no matter how much you love me, you must go. And no matter how much I love you, you'd better stay. What am I saying? Oh, for heaven's sake, beat it, before it's too late. What are you doing? I can't live without you, come back. Why are you standing there? Don't listen to me! Just go! Oh, damn it! So what's wrong with strawberries and whipped cream? Oh, Jim, you've been right all along. We are made for each other. I want you to tell your little biscuit to go to hell! (*SHE looks around.*) Jim? Jim? Where are you? How do you like that—the bastard walked out on me! I can never understand—why they always do.

A CIVILIZED LUNCH WITH A CIVILIZED LADY

Serious

I do believe in being civilized, don't you? But, of course you do, or we wouldn't be having this civilized lunch. Another white wine, waiter, and another martini for my friend. Austin drinks martinis, but you know that. I never could. I tried once—to keep up with him—but I became terribly drunk in front of his boss. Quite uncivilized and I don't think Austin has ever forgiven me. Even when I learned about you, I tried to be a good sport. And, oh, my dear, I can't thank you enough for being so discreet. I minded, I suppose, but as long as he remembered my birthday, honored our anniversary, took me to my favorite restaurants and acted—like a devoted husband should, it seemed sporting enough. Cheers. I don't wish to embarrass you, but I've always loved Austin, in my quiet, civilized way. However, when it came to—our intimate life—how can I properly explain it? Oh, I forgot, you would know about that, too. How delightful, I have someone to discuss embarrassing things with, without actually saying things and thus becoming vulgar. Another white wine, waiter, and another martini for my delightful, understanding friend. We did have fun, you know, Austin and I. The theatre on Thursdays, Tuesday night tickets for the ballet, and weekends in The Hamptons, reading. It was just quiet fun. Do you have fun with Austin, or do you—Oh, please forgive me. How impertinent of me to ask you about your private life, even if it is with my husband. Cheers. Austin I'm sure is going to make you very happy, and now that we've met, I know you will make him happy as well, and after all, that's what truly matters in life. One can't stand in the way of other people's happiness, now can one? Shall we order? Have something delicious. I suggest beginning with the scallops en brochette. Austin's favorite, but—of course—you—would know that too. Oh, please forgive me. Just a brief and embarrassing—if not trashy—show of emotion. You see, I've gotten so used to Austin, and I'm afraid I'm going to feel—a bit at sea for some time. My fault, I fear. No one ever prepared me—nor could I ever imagine—that anything like this would ever happen. It's going to take a little time I'm afraid, for me to—become accustomed—to realize—to understand properly that—Oh, yes, waiter, we will order the scallops en brochette for my friend. They are truly delicious here. Oh, but, of course, I'm being presumptuous. You already know that.

A PLAYWRIGHT'S WIFE WAITS FOR THE OPENING NIGHT REVIEWS

Comic

No, George, I don't want your play to be a hit tonight. I have struggled with you for the past fifteen years to improve my mental health. It's true, when we were first married, I wasn't prepared for your first hit, but what was worse was that your first hit didn't prepare me for the six dreary little rotten flops that followed. Then no more gowns from Saks. No more trinkets from Cartier's. I didn't mind that so much, but after living on Park Avenue, oh, how I hated Hoboken. When you think what you subjected me to all these years. Reading your dreary plays till four in the morning, only to be awakened by you at seven to tell me about a brilliant new idea. Taking your abuse when I thought they were bad. Taking your abuse when I thought they were good. Typing your messy scripts till dawn. Then I would see you tear them up that afternoon, only to have you decide I was right and you were wrong—and then I had to type them up all over again! And why am I here? Because every opening night after the deadly reviews come in, you threaten to jump. And if you have another flop they will be wiping you up from the sidewalk. Last time as I held you back from the window I almost fell myself. But you have been nice this time, dedicating your play to me. Since it is about me. Two acts about a wife who is driven by an egomaniacal, self-destructive husband who is slowly and savagely tormenting her through agonizing torture, until she is driven to her self-inflicted crucifixion. Before I married you, I was a sweet innocent young girl who thought marrying an accountant exciting. But who could have prepared me for you? Ah! The television reviews are about to air. This time I'm going to leave you alone and go to a bar across the street. Since this play symbolizes our marriage, jump, George. You won't even have to wait for the reviews. Jump!

WEDDINGS CAN BE FATAL FOR MOTHERS

Comic

Oh, Mabel, me nervous? What is there to be nervous about? It's just an everyday occurrence. My daughter is getting married within the hour, while my other daughter, who refuses to get married, is going to have her baby any minute. Plus the fact that I have to be nice to my husband, who has run away with another woman. Upset? What is there to be upset about? (*SHE laughs.*) I've only planned this wedding once, called it off once, then planned it all over again. And as for my other daughter's wedding, I've only planned that one twice. And called it off twice—even though she is pregnant. You don't know how much fun I've been having. Sending out all the invitations, sending out all the cancellations, making all the explanations, and then sending out all the invitations again. What fun! And then with my other daughter; sending out all the invitations, sending out all the cancellations, making all the explanations—twice! Not to mention all the presents going back and forth, back and forth—so senseless, plus all the postage. (*SHE turns.*) Oh, there's my beautiful daughter. Susan, darling, you look so lovely, doesn't she, Mabel? After sending back your wedding dress five times, you finally picked the right one. What? What? No. No! I don't think she said that. No. She didn't say that. Did she say that, Mabel? She didn't say that, did she? Now, Susan, darling, I don't think you understand. There are two hundred people waiting at the church and if you don't show up, it will ruin their day. What do you mean, you don't want to? Of course you want to. You're just over-reacting because you're so happy. Isn't that so, Mabel? And listen ... Jill is screaming because she's so happy. What? What? No. No. I don't think you said that, Mabel. No, you didn't say that, Mabel, did you? (*SHE turns again.*) Now, Jill, darling, you can't have your baby now, not until your sister gets married, and since she refuses to get married, why don't you get married instead? No one will mind. Everyone is so confused, they won't care. Who cares if he's your sister's fiance? I don't care, and if I don't care, he won't care. What, Mabel? Who's hysterical? I'm not hysterical. All I know is that today, someone has to get married. Why don't you get married, Mabel? Maybe my husband will get married. Maybe I'll get married all over again. No, Mabel I'm really all right. I like standing up here on the table. It puts everything into perspective. You know what, Mabel? All this is my fault. I should have never become a mother. (*SHE screams.*)

AN UNSOPHISTICATED WIFE WANTS A DIVORCE AND A LITTLE MORE

Comic

You think you're superior to me, don't you, Phil? Because your family is in the blue book and I barely made the white pages. You think you're superior because you grew up in that mansion in Atlanta, while I grew up in Wyoming. Well, let me tell you, Phil, that mansion you grew up in has termites. Oh, yes, it does; it has termites. I used to hate to go there, Phil. Every time we'd have dinner everyone would sit around the dinner table and talk about your sisters' coming out parties. And then, they would look at me. Well, I mean—how can you come out when you come from Wyoming? At least, when I was in Wyoming, I was calm. I never raised my voice once. In fact, I never talked much. People don't talk much in Wyoming. We look at TV instead. Now look at me. I'm a nervous wreck. I can't take your lifestyle anymore. Dinners at the country club, ballooning in France. A villa over there, a mansion over here, a penthouse up there. And I'm sick and tired of hearing you talk about your days at Oxford and soccer. Bragging about how great you were when you made the team. Except I found out the truth, and I'm hysterical enough to tell all. The truth is, they threw you off the team at Oxford. Oh, yes, they did. Because of that afternoon when you got the ball, and lost your sense of direction and scored for the other side. So—I want a divorce, Phil. A simple divorce. I want the mansion in Atlanta, the membership at the club, the penthouse, and what is over there and what is over here. Because after living this intolerable life with you, how can I go back to Wyoming? You ruined me, Phil. I've grown accustomed to the good life. And for that, I shall never forgive you!

HER COLLEGE LOVER TAKES HER HOME TO MEET MOTHER

Serious

Oh—it's been some weekend all right. The big weekend when the guy brings the girl home to meet his mother. I can't thank you for all you have done, Mrs. Winslow. Oh, I forgot, Samantha. Now that the weekend is over I want to tell you something. I think it's real dumb for me to call you Samantha. I know it's supposed to be sophisticated for me to call you Samantha, but by now you know how unsophisticated I am. I can't tell you how nice you have been to point out in your subtle way how different your son's life is from mine. And if you mention the word breeding once more, I think I will throw up all over your seventeenth century Persian rug. No, I don't ride horses, and I have never eaten snails, and I think the game of croquet is dumb, too. High spirited, you called me. I'm sure you meant awkward. Enthusiastic, you said. Loud is what you meant. Simple and fresh. That was a nice way to remind me of my naivete. You pulled out all the stops to make me feel out of place and uncomfortable. And do you want to know the truth? You succeeded. This weekend has been a nightmare because I so desperately wanted to make a good impression. But you made up your mind about me before I came, when you couldn't find my name in the blue book. My mother works in a department store, to get the discount, and my father is a laborer. Out-of-work laborer, that is. And the only reason I'm in the same prestigious university as your son, is because I am financially deprived. Those were your words. I'd rather say broke. But, you see, Mrs. Winslow, I'm not deprived. I've got what it takes to be where I am. You paid for your son's tuition. I earned mine. And because of that, he's proud of me. But at this moment I don't have much pride left. I never thought anyone could intimidate me, but you certainly have. You see—it's all very simple. I wanted your approval because of how I feel about your son. I tried not to embarrass him, while I tried to please you, and somewhere I lost myself. Before I came, I bought that stupid dress. You called it quaint. I felt like an elephant in a sarong. I should have worn my sweat shirt with SOCK IT TO ME written across my chest. No wonder your son has been so nervous all weekend. Your son. How about that? I can't even say his name in front of you. It's because he's two different people, trying to be one. This weekend has been a waste of time. And boring. So boring. And sad. Your son brought me home to meet you. What a chance he took, and he lost. He lost, or perhaps you did. And what you fear the most, Mrs. Winslow, or should I say, Samantha—my marrying into your family—don't worry about it, because after this weekend—you will be the last to know.

A NERVOUS ACTRESS AUDITIONS

Comic

Nervous? Me nervous? Oh, I'm not nervous. What is there to be nervous about? This is just an audition. I either get the part or I don't. What's that? Just life and death. Oh, you want me to begin. Sure, why not? Why do I see all these spots? I see all these spots dancing around me. Don't worry out there, I'll be all right as soon as all these spots go away. Go away, damn spots. Oh, good, I can see again. What? Oh, you want me to begin. I will. I promise I will. As soon as I can start breathing. And then I promise I'll begin, except at the moment I can't breathe. In. Out. In. Out. I think I'm breathing again. OK, let's go. I'm as calm as a rattlesnake in heat. Wait a minute, I think I'm going to have a heart attack. I'll be with you as soon as I have a heart attack. Except, my heart has stopped beating, and any fool knows that your heart has to be beating in order for it to stop when you have a heart attack. What? OK. Anything you say. I'm ready to read Lady Macbeth. Cold. (*SHE clears her throat.*) "Out, damn spot!" I think I said something like that already. "Out—comma—capital I—I say—exclamation point—dash—Hell is murky—exclamation point. Fie—comma—my lord—comma—fie—exclamation point. A soldier—comma—and afeard?" Afeard? Excuse me, but there's a typo here. It should be "afraid." What am I doing? I'm reading Lady Macbeth. It's just that I've had to take this job proofreading, and lately it's become a habit. Oh, thanks a lot. You've been awfully kind. Now all I have to do is get off the stage.

NO MORE CHORUS LINES FOR HER

Serio-comic

Hi, Pops! What a day for an audition. Blizzard or not, when it comes to actors, they all show up. Thirty-three years you've been at this stage door, seeing us come and go. Mainly go. Oh, my God, why wasn't I that smart? Fifteen years in the chorus and I can't get a real part. Singin' and dancin' night after night, in hits and in flops. What a stupid jerk I was. Do ya know what I thought when I first became a gypsy? I thought I would become a star. Right in this very theatre, on that very stage. (*SHE throws her head back and laughs.*) Dumb jerk! You know, Pops, I'm getting too old for the chorus. Yeah, I know I'm the best, but the last time you shoulda' seen me huffin' and puffin'. Ten times during that show I could hardly get through the last act. Hell, most of the time I just moved my lips. If anyone thinks I'm gonna do all that razzamatazz, and sing at the same time, they're crazy. They shoulda' fired me. What am I talkin' about—they did. That last night I kicked so high and sang so loud, I upstaged the friggin' star. The kids gave me a Tiffany watch—how about that? Engraved, "To Toby, The Best Gypsy on Broadway." (*SHE turns.*) This is the third time Gino has called me back. Oh, Pops, just think: a solo out on that stage—all by myself. One dance number with all those friggin' gypsies behind me for a change, kickin' their legs until it hurts. And a scene of my own. Toby Talks! (*SHE turns.*) Gino owes me one. Last year he begged me to go out on that lousy bus and truck tour—me!—the best gypsy on Broadway! He needed me to teach those kids all my tricks. So he owes me one. Who am I kiddin'? I went out on that tour because I was turned down for every chorus line in the past two years. And you wanna know who beat me out? A lot of friggin' gypsies I've taught over the years. Next time, I'm gonna keep my secrets to myself. (*SHE hugs her script to her.)* I gotta get this part. It's only fair. God knows, I've paid my dues. It would only be right. Because this is where it all began—right out there on that stage. I've come full circle. A stupid kid who sang and danced her heart out, thinking she'd become a star. A worn-out gypsy who desperately needs a part because there's no chorus line waitin' for her anymore. Oh, well, let's get this friggin' thing over with. (*SHE starts to walk off.*) See ya later, pal!

A WOMAN COMES BACK TO THE SCENE OF THE CRIME

Serious

Oh, it's quite all right. Really it is. You can use the word *kill* in front of me. Oh, yes, you can. Because, you see, I didn't kill her. Now, now, I know you know that. But it's strange—when everyone around you tells you that you did—over the years you begin to believe it. The jury said I did. The prosecuting attorney—the press—everyone. (*SHE turns to them.*) Except the two of you ... Of course, I want to stay here. Don't you see? That's why I had to come back. (*SHE whispers.*) To the scene of the crime, so to speak ... Now, stop. It did happen. That's a fact. But when I look around this room, I don't just remember that one night. I remember all sorts of things. The times we spent together. All those years. Those lovely dinners. Wonderful summers. The memories in this room have become a part of me. Oh—I can't believe I'm finally free. (*SHE turns away from them.*) Prison. At night when all the lights would go out, I would lie there listening—to screams—or moans—or somebody being sick. I would try to go to sleep, but I'd be awakened by that endless noise that I could never get away from. Then—the bell would ring, and it would be morning. Again and again. Day after day. Week after week. Nothing would ever change. As the years went by—along with my life—endlessly. (*SHE quickly turns to them.*) Oh, no, you can't forget. Oh, no—I can't do that. It would be wrong. I have to remember it all—and deal with it in my own way. (*SHE laughs.*) You see—I'm not shaking. My heart is not pounding. You look surprised; you shouldn't be. I've had a long time to get over it. Don't you see—I haven't come back to dwell on the past. I've come back to begin again. And I can't thank you enough for giving me this second chance. And—(*SHE laughs.*) I would like another glass of champagne. (*SHE looks at them for a moment.*) What's wrong? You look worried.

AN ECCENTRIC NEIGHBOR TALKS TOO MUCH

Comic

Yoo, hoo! Anyone home? Oh, there you are. I hope I'm not intruding. Here's your meatloaf. I now you don't know who I am. I'm Mrs. La Salle, your neighbor. I saw you move in. My house is the closest to yours. You see—it's way down there. It took me at least fifteen minutes to come. I walk. I won't go into anything on wheels. Well, I couldn't let you move in without welcoming you, now could I? I hope you like my meatloaf. I give it to all the new people. *(SHE looks around.)* Oh, what a sweet house this is. It's absolutely adorable. I've always wanted to live here. You see, I want to get away from my wretched sister. She's mean to me. She won't give me any money. So, any dummy knows I could never move away. Well, isn't this nice. Someone has finally moved into this old house. The others told me not to come. But why shouldn't I? I said to myself. I'm not an old fraidy cat. Oh, my dears, the others don't even like to pass the house. But, I said to my horrid sister, "This will give me the chance to peek into that strange house with the mysterious lights." Did I say mysterious lights? I didn't mean to. I'm sure you will be very happy here—once you get used to everything. Some nights, when I can't go to sleep, I go out on my balcony and watch it. Do you know, my dears, when the moon is high, you can see a strange, beautiful woman dancing in the garden. And a man sitting up in a tree. No one believes me when I tell them. Some people go so far as to say I'm crazy. Of course we all know that isn't so. However, even my dreadful sister has to admit this house is haunted. Oh, my dear! Oh, my goodness! I said it. Now, I just feel awful. By the way *(SHE whispers.)* have you seen them? The ghosts, of course! Well, I can tell you one thing, I'd rather live with ghosts than with my sister. Oh, I'm so glad someone has finally moved in here. This house should be filled with people. Now, I really must go, or my sister will crucify me. I do hope you like my meatloaf. And by the way, if you do see them, say hello to them for me. Maybe they would like me to make them a meatloaf. Ta-ta, my dears. (*SHE looks around.*) And ta-ta, to you, too.

CAN A WIFE GIVE TOO MUCH TO HER HUSBAND?

Comic

What do you want from me, Frank? Just tell me what, and I'll give it to you. Moral support, you have it. Love, it's always been there. Sex, whenever you want. Money, what I have is yours. You used to tell me what you wanted. It was easy that way. Then I always knew where I stood. Do you want to have an affair, Frank? So go—have your affair. Come back. Have an affair with your wife. Did I ever mind? What do you want, Frank? Do you want to quit your job? So—quit. Live off me for awhile. I'm saying awhile, not forever. Do you want to move? We'll move. I don't care where the hell I live as long as you're there and—you don't have to be there all the time. So—what do you want from me? A baby? I think it may be too late, but if you want to have a baby, I'll suffer through one for you. Or we'll adopt. So, I'll be a mother and work and be your wife. Worse things could happen. What do you want from me, Frank? Just let me know. It's done. Say the word and I'll drop dead. And if you want it done tomorrow, I'll do it today. And if I don't like it I'll smile. So what do you want? You want me to change? I'll be a redhead. All it takes is an hour. You want me to talk different. I'll get a speech coach. Less sophisticated, more sophisticated—I can go either way. So why don't you open your mouth and talk? By now you should know I'm a very easy person to get along with. Maybe you want to commit suicide. Try it. I'll be there to bring you back to life. Maybe you want to make love to a man. Hey—so what? Then you'll enjoy me even more. A threesome. You want a threesome? Is that what you want, Frank? I'll do anything once. Anything, anything. But you've got to tell me to do something. You want a divorce. You have it. We'll live together in sin. Or maybe you want to live with someone else. Live with her, and pay me long visits. I'm very flexible, Frank. I'm easygoing, to say the least. But I've got to know what you want or

I'll go crazy. And if that's what you want—look at me. You've succeeded. So—let me know, Frank. (*Pause.*) I see. I see. I make you feel guilty. I see. I see. Oh, Frank, I don't know—what to do about that.

A MOTHER SHOCKS HER DAUGHTER AFTER SEEING A SHRINK

Comic

Now, darling, your mother is just bursting with news, but before I tell you what has happened, I would appreciate it if you would make me a martini. I know it's ten in the morning. I know I never drink martinis. I know they make me sick. It's a test, my dear, to see if I'm cured. Now, don't look at me as if I've gone crazy. I've been seeing a shrink, instead. And it's all because of your father. You see—on our honeymoon we went on a cruise to the islands. We spent our wedding night on the ship. The sea could not have been calmer. I drank my martini, as was my custom, and I got deathly sick. I had to spend my entire wedding night in the bathroom. And I've never been able to drink another martini since. What do you mean—so? Surely, you must see the deep, underlying significance. Transference, of course! The sea did not make me sick. The martini did not make me sick. It was your father who made me sick! And it has taken me two years working with my shrink to understand that. Now, if only I could drink another martini again, I will be cured. Oh. I'm so nervous, I'm trembling all over. (*SHE holds up a glass.*) Better get a wastebasket just in case I'm not cured. Here's to my shrink. If it doesn't work, I'm going to sue him for malpractice. (*SHE drinks the martini.*) Success! Now, I can divorce your father. Why are you so shocked? Just because I've gotten along with him, doesn't mean I have to live with him. Get me another martini! Drunk? Oh, yes! Drunk with joy! Drunk with life! A new beginning! Don't you see? On my wedding night, I spent the entire night in the bathroom, because way down deep, I didn't want to come out of the bathroom and face the fact that I had married your father. Of course we are happy together, but a lot of trash has gone under the bridge in the last years. And it's about time I jumped into a new river. Now let's talk about you. When you rented this apartment, I must say I was concerned. I thought you would go wild. Go too far. Well, now that I've seen my shrink, I don't think you have gone far enough. I know what you've been doing. You've been watching too much television, that's what you've been doing. Get out is what I say! Experience life to its fullest! And don't be afraid of the consequences. Oh, my dear. You're not talking to your old mother. So, you've been doing a little of this and a little of that. I've been liberated. Break out the pot!

THE LADY HAS EVERYTHING

Comic

Oh, Mildred, why am I so talented? I was cursed the moment I was born. To be parented not only by a wealthy father, but also a rich mother, is too much to bear. I not only take after my father, who is absolutely brilliant, but I also take after my mother, who is devastatingly stunning. It's really irritating. I didn't mind being a child genius, but to grow up and become an internationally famous author is outrageous. And for all my books to make *The Times* best seller list is one thing, but for them to stay number one for a year is depressing. Life is hell. But I'll tell you, what really gets me down is when they make them into movies. All those humiliating awards, and who needs oodles of money? And why am I so witty, witty all the time? It's embarrassing to get more laughs than Johnny Carson. Whatever I say, the audience can't stop laughing. No wonder Johnny doesn't want me on his show anymore. Do you blame him? Now, my dear, you know very well I try not to be appealing to men. In fact, I go out of my way to discourage them from adoring me. But they can't help themselves, poor darlings. And when I say no, they all threaten to kill themselves. And when I say yes, why do they have to buy me yachts? And propose marriage? It's enough to drive a woman to drink. And do they all have to be devastatingly handsome, unbearably manly and titled? And why is it when I walk into a room they all pick on me? Enough, I say. Give another woman a chance. My life is grotesque. I don't even get wrinkles. My hairdresser told me he can't do a thing with my hair because it's absolutely perfect. And no matter what I eat, I never gain a pound, and if I don't eat, I keep my voluptuous shape. So it's useless. Oh, Mildred, it's hell to be me. Why? You josh. Because, my dear, I'm so wonderful, I bore myself. But what's even worse, I'll never know if I'm adored for the real me.

A LOVER COMES BACK

Serious

A confession? In the middle of the night in a beach cottage with the fog rolling in? It sounds frightening and a little melodramatic. No, Jack, you don't have to tell me you love me. I must say, when you came up here without any warning, without telephoning, you caught me off guard. After all these years, I was hoping you would look old. Worn out. Dissipated. At least bald. And then I turned, and there you were. You hadn't changed at all. My defenses were down. Maybe if I had been prepared, it would have been different. I couldn't help but think of that summer Cynthia and you and I all rented that dilapidated beach cottage up here. At the end of that summer, that's when you told me. That you were going to marry Cynthia. And that's when I began to dramatically walk the dunes at night, feeling sorry for myself. But when I was so dramatically walking those dunes, I suddenly asked myself a question. What would happen to you if I married you? I laughed out loud. You would be bald by now. You always looked shaggy, but never shabby. You would have grown to hate me, because you were born with a silver spoon in your mouth without the cash to buy the groceries. So—you married Cynthia because of the groceries. There's nothing wrong with that. And now you have money of your own. And now Cynthia wants a divorce. Oh, it's you who wants a divorce. Well, what does it matter? You're a free man again. In demand, I would think. Handsome. Intelligent. And fun. Do you know what you are? (*SHE laughs.*) You're a little school boy in a candy store and you want everything. Maybe that's why I've always adored you. And, without warning, you're back here again. And I do believe you. I know you love me—then and now. Maybe confessions should be made in the middle of the night, in a beach cottage with the fog rolling in. Oh, my darling, this is so hard for me to say. I know what a terrible sacrifice I'm making. But, you see, in you came and my defenses were down and I realized for the first time what a son of a bitch you really are. So go back to New York. Go back to Cynthia. While you're at it, why don't you just go to hell?

SHE'S A KOOK AND SHE KNOWS IT

Comic

Do you always kiss like that? So thoroughly and completely and overwhelmingly. Do you know what I want to do right away, this instant, before the thrill is gone? I have this overwhelming desire—to bake a lemon chiffon pie for you. That is, if I could, but you see, I can't. Oh, dear, everything is happening so fast for me. One thing always happens after the other in my life. It keeps piling up, like a snowball speeding down an enormous hill during summer. And if I did have an affair with you, I would only be left with the slush. I'm not good at things like this. And the best thing for me to do is to stay away from men who have brown watery eyes like yours. I'm very bad at playing games with men. That's why no man would even dream of asking me to marry him. Some women are so good at playing games. Not me. I always lose at checkers. And in Monopoly, no one ever stops at my hotels. Of course, men take me to hotels all the time—but that's not the same thing as winning. If you're confused, then just think how confused I am. I crave things that are bad for me—like you. I'm a child who eats too much candy, feels sick in the morning and then begs for a chocolate bar. Most women are so sure of themselves. I envy them. I always go home too late, say the wrong things because no one else is talking. I fill in the gaps. I have a knack of putting the finishing touch on every party. I'm the hangover. You see, I'm like a ghost. Sometimes I don't think I'm real. It's only when the lights are low and the candles lit that I can create my magic. Put me in a kitchen and you have to call out the fire department. Anyone can eat burned soft-boiled eggs at two in the morning and find it charming. Try that at seven, it becomes trying. So, you see, if you kissed me again like you did before, I would only want to bake a lemon chiffon pie for you. Except now we both know I can't . And instead of that I will end up in bed with you. But when morning comes, don't expect me to be there. I vanish. I'm like a ghost. Sad, isn't it?

A PERFECT MOTHER-IN-LAW, AN IMPERFECT MOTHER

Comic

Oh, Pamela—don't move. Just stay the way you are. Let me look at you for a second. It's so good to see you, after all these years. One of the happiest moments of my life, was when you divorced my son. Since then, Steven's been miserable. I've been delighted. What do you think of my huge house? Ostentatious, isn't it? But I said to myself, everyone flaunts it these days so why shouldn't I? I am able to afford this monstrosity because I finally came into my inheritance. My father thought I would squander it away—so he stipulated in his will when I was to receive it. He never thought I would live this long. You see—we all die young in our family. So reassuring that Steven is not long for this world. Have some champagne, Dom Perignon, I drink nothing else. And spoon up the caviar. Beluga, direct from the Black Sea. I've decided to spend everything I have so Steven won't inherit a sou. Now—surely you still can't be in love with him. I mean, what is there to love? He's an obnoxious, dreadful man, and I have a right to say that since I'm his mother. That's why I never wanted him to marry you. I didn't want him to ruin your life. What he needs is a real bitch. Someone who will take him for all he's got. Like me. What do you mean he's not that bad? He couldn't be worse. I should have done him in when he was two. At that age sons are so trusting; after that, forget it. Scram, I say. Get yourself a bikini, or whatever they're not wearing these days, and find yourself a beautiful young man. Have yourself a fling, then meet a banker and marry him. What? But that's treachery! Do you mean you've been seeing Steven? What? That's heresy! Do you mean you're going back to him? What? That's absurd! Do you mean you're going to have his baby? Oh, Pamela, where's your responsibility to mankind? How could you bring another Steven into this world? And what is worse—make me a grandmother. I'm so disappointed in you. You're not the woman I thought you were. And if you make my son happy—I shall never forgive you.

A WOMAN REMEMBERS, PROMISES BROKEN

Serious

Sandwich, John? Let me make you a big ham sandwich, just the way you like it. There. You're doing it again. Staring in front of you—blank like. Slipping away. I know you're tired. They shouldn't give you the early sessions, then you could sleep late. I saw the house again today. It's such a beautiful house. I've fallen in love with it. There's a tree in the back yard. The lady told me it's over a hundred years old. Imagine that. It has a real porch. And upstairs, from the bedroom, you can see the garden. It's not much of a garden to speak of, but it's better than none, and it does have flagstones. Oh! And the staircase, John—it's so graceful—it turns at the bottom. We won't even have to buy a new refrigerator. I measured this old one and it fits in nicely. This time I have to have my house. We could afford it if you would cash in the bonds. Can't? You mean won't! I've always done without. Don't you see—this would make the difference. It's what I need to make me happy. Then, maybe I wouldn't—it's just that nothing has ever changed for me all these years. I feel as if I've gone nowhere, since the day we came. That's not true. You could be principal today. You turned that job down deliberately, didn't you? Deliberately! Well, I don't care what you say, this time I'm going to get my house! Oh, John, what has happened to you? Silence. Always, silence. At night when you're next to me, I can almost feel the silence. And I begin to think about all the years You weren't like this in the beginning. (*SHE turns.*) Johnny, I'm so happy. Did you see all my friends at the wedding? They were green with envy. It's not every day a woman can marry a man as handsome and as educated as you. My, my. Superintendent of schools! Now, hush, Johnny, my head is spinning. Papa used to tell me I was the most beautiful thing in his life. He was so happy with Mama. Sometimes I felt left out. Yet, I knew what he meant. You don't know what it's like to have so little for such a long time. The lovely things in you begin to dry up. That's the worst, you know, to feel yourself dying, surrounded by other people's happiness. But now! I'm finally reaching out! At last, a world all my own! Oh, Johnny, tell me again—how wonderful it's all going to be. (*SHE turns.*) You always thought you were better than my father, didn't you, John? But unlike you, he was a man you could respect. There were promises made! Promises broken! What? It s just iced tea, John. Suspicious!

THE GIRL IS THROWN OUT, THE WOMAN COMES HOME

Serious

Ten years ago, you threw me out of this house, Mom. You gave me some money, didn't even see me to the bus, and I haven't heard from you since. You said, "There's no excuse for what you did. I don't want you in my house." And I remember how you said it. As if you were talking to a stranger. "Go to him," you said, "he got you pregnant." I told you I didn't know where he was, but you didn't hear me because you didn't want to. Instead you gave me a lecture. Told me what a pity I wasn't more like my sister. We had different aspirations. She wanted to get married, I wanted to be somebody. "So go," you said. "Go for a nice ride on your high horse. I would be ashamed to walk down the street with you." Sally got married. A perfect marriage. And while she was having her little girl, surrounded by love and affection, I gave birth to my son. Alone. I wrote you. But you never answered. I know how you felt about me, but how could you not care for your own grandson? And he's your grandson all right, and as long as I am in this house you will treat him like one. I don't know what I would have done if it wasn't for Sally. She used to come and see me all the time without your knowing, because you wouldn't approve. And as our children played together, do you know what we always talked about? You! She was my only link to you. And as the years went by I fought like hell to become the person I knew I could be. My fashions are worn by thousands of women across the country and in Europe. And Sally all the time gave me moral support, and when I became a success she was so proud. And when she finally told you, I understand you changed the subject. I became what you thought I wouldn't! And you hated me for that, too. And then Sally stopped crying. I wondered why. It was Jim who finally told me. He said you didn't want to me know. I took the next plane out and ran to that hospital only to be told I was too late. You even cheated me out of that! I don't care how you feel about me, but she was my sister and I had a right to know! So—go ahead. Cry! Cry as much as you want! Cry with me! We both lost the person we loved most. You know, it's as if Sally had known. It's as if she had.

NOT OF LEGAL AGE

Serio-comic

Shit! What do ya think I'm doin? I'm waitin' for the train to come so I can heat it. Who knows when the train will come, but one will come. Ya have to flag it down, that's what ya have to do in this stinkin' town because no self respectin' train would ever stop here. Shit! I'm not as old as ya think. I'm not legal yet, but I've done everything that you can do when ya become legal. I drunk rye whiskey with beer chasers until I puked. Had all kinds of sex with the youngies and the oldies and it don't matter to me as long as I get what's comin' and what is rightful mine. I take after my mama. Shit! She was a real good one down deep. Don't know why she had to die on me like that and leave me alone. I asked her not to die. Shit ! No one's goin' to get what's rightful mine. And I'm holdin' the potato sack for dear life and I will never let it go, even when I sleep, because everyone is no good and everyone will cheat me blind. That's how it is. So, what do ya want with me, Mister? Huh? What do ya want? Ya not breathin' down my neck to give me a good farewell. That's a pretty big bill ya got in your hand and I don't mind takin, it. But I've gotta tell ya, I've done a lot but I'm not that good. So—what do ya want, Mister? So what if ya knew my mama, so what? What do ya want with me, Mister—because I'm takin' that bill and where I'm gonna put it, ya never gonna see it again. So, what do ya want? Nothin? Everyone wants somethin'. All Mama wanted was to have some fun and she gave a lot of fun to a lot of people—for a rightful price. Everything has a price. I don't know how much I'm gonna have to pay to be happy. I bet a lot. I wonder how much I'm gonna have to pay to be somebody. I bet a lot. Well, I better get some big bills like that, wave down that train that's comin' from someplace good and goin' to someplace better. Shit! No wonder ya have to wave it down for it to stop here. Hey, Mister, come back. I owe ya. Hey, Mister, why are ya leavin' me with this big bill? Hey, Mister, what's wrong with ya, anyway? Jerk. Dumb, stupid, jerko. Mama, I wish ya was here. I'm not legal yet and I don't know nothin'. I don't know what's out there. And, Mama, this jerko gave me the biggest bill I ever did see for no reason at all. Shit! He's gonna come back and get what he wants. And if he don't—if he don't come back—then, Mama, there's a lot of crazy people out there. Wowee!

THE UNKNOWN

Serious

Do you really want to know who *they* are? Are you sure? Who I think *they* are. These intruders from God knows where? If you want then I will tell you. (*Pause.*) They are little green people, or purple ones with polka-dot faces, or no faces at all. Don't laugh! They come from planets or from other places like under the sea. They are figures that fly or walk in ways we don't understand. They don't wish to be seen or else they would come up to us and say, "Why don't we go for a Big Mac and a shake." You smile. Or perhaps they are complicated thought, electrical in nature, caught in an electro-magnetic field. And since they can't go anywhere they stay here with us like ghosts, haunting the world, preferring L.A. or New York. Or maybe they are the unknown factor: X, Y, or Z. Or not at all plural but one. One mind, plural in nature, but one. Like the Father, the Son and the Holy Ghost. Back to ghosts again that haunt us. Or not male but female, like Mother, Daughter and infant girl so tender and mild. Or they are Gods that preceded all other Gods, before there was a world, before there was a universe. And they have come to tell us that our Gods are unmerciful and cruel. That our lives are unfair and restricting. That our nature is pure but we are polluted by outmoded thought and insatiable greed and the need for power. And they want us to come back to the time when it all began, so that they can wash away the centuries of corrosion that has damaged our brains. *(In a whisper.)* Or maybe they don't exist at all. And they could simply be part of ourselves, the stranger, darker part of each of us, the part that lives in the backyards of our innermost private mind. (*Loud.*) Or they are something planned, or something the stars made, or something unexpected like a sun bursting into flames and the fragments of the sun becoming cold, and wanting to live—they need our warmth, our light. And they come from the star, Algol, that cruel star that brings about violence. That fixed star, 26 degrees Taurus. A star that causes those whose sun is in aspect—to go berserk. (*Quiet.*) Or, maybe they have tails. And they follow each other's tails and go around and around and they cannot stop. And so—they go wildly around in an endless circle that takes them nowhere. But wanting to stop, needing to stop; the only way they can stop, is to unite us. Control us, so that all our frantic energy become theirs. And finally they can rest and, having learned all about circles and tails, they can use their superior knowledge and teach us about circles and our tails and what it is all about in the first place. (*Pause.*) You're not laughing anymore. You're not smiling. That's who I think *they* are.

MARRIAGE IS NOT ENOUGH

Serious

It's a lovely gift. It really is. And extravagant. A gold brooch with a sapphire in it. Last year for my birthday you gave me an electric can opener. Oh, yes, yes, I did like it and needed it. The old one could barely open a can of Del Monte tomato sauce. And a trip to Paris. Last year we went camping in the Poconos—as we did the year before and as long as I can remember, except for the time we went to Bermuda and that was because we were on our honeymoon. You really didn't have to do all this. I know you love me. You never have to tell me. Or show me for that matter. Nor did you ever. Oh, God! Why did you have to do all this? It only makes it worse. More difficult. I have something to tell you, Bill, and the strange thing is I know you're not going to believe me. Most men would, but strangely, not you. So—I might as well blurt it out and confess. I'm seeing another man, Bill. No, that's not nice. Let me make it plainer. I'm going out with another man. No, Archibald only takes me for an ice cream soda after we rehearse at the little theatre. That's not what I mean. So let me spell it out as clearly as I can. I'm having an affair with another man and that means I'm having sex with him, too. What do you mean, I'm too old? Bill, I'm only late thirties—early forties. And for the first time in a long time, I feel attractive. And he's attractive, too. I mean—he's as attractive as you, but with him—it's different. I know you think it's always the same, but it's not always the same. Now, Bill, don't get me wrong, we've had a—how can I say it—we've had a nice life together. Nice, that's how it's been. Uneventful, dull, but nice. And what did I know? I thought it was nice. Now nice is not good enough. And you must have suspected this was happening, or you wouldn't have bought me that brooch, or wanted to take me to Paris. Well, I suppose you're right. When a man sees his wife holding hands with another man while he nibbles on her ear, he must know something's up. But you think I'm going to get over this, don't you? I can't, Bill. I can't because I don't want to. I don't even know how this is going to turn out. I only know I've never felt like this in my entire life. And no matter what, I've got to take this chance. Once? Just once? I know you will never understand because you don't know what I feel. It's wonderful, Bill. It's everything I thought it would be, but like nothing I've ever experienced. So—cash in the plane tickets. And take the brooch back to the jeweler. What would we do in Paris, anyway? And the brooch would only stay in my jewelry case, along with the pearls you gave me when we were married. That's not for us. But there is something else, and that's why I'm going to go through with this. And if it doesn't work out, and I'm still here next year for my birthday, and you still want me—that's when you can buy me that electric blanket.

IN THE EXECUTIVE JUNGLE

Serious

Well, I did it! In fact, dear Trevor, and I'm sure this will make your blood run cold, Benson promised me a contract by this afternoon. So—no take-over, Trevor. Benson's contract has saved my hide. We're in a business where sharks eat sharks, but I've never played that game; I've always kept my pride and my dignity. It's irritated you, that, and my being a woman. I know how you love to play with people and see them squirm. That's the reason you introduced me to Benson. You knew how I could get that contract but you didn't think I would do it. Certainly not the Grace Kelly of the business world. Mistake. One night in bed with a stranger doesn't make me a whore. So—go and tell your dirty story in all the board rooms on the Street. The fact is, dear Trevor, no one will believe you. You've underestimated me. I'm as tough as you, but thank God, not as ruthless. I don't belong in your club. I won without joining. Good morning, Trevor. No, please, don't call your chauffeur—I'll walk. (*SHE begins to leave, then suddenly stops.*) You really set me up. (*SHE closes her eyes.*) Well, Trevor, aren't you going to ask your chauffeur how good I was last night? Or, have you already? I think you can have him leave now. (*SHE turns.*) So—you have me exactly where you want me. I will be the laugh of Wall Street before the market closes, and by tonight you will own my company. So—that means I'm working for you now. Teach me, Trevor. Teach me everything you know. Show me the tricks. And if you want me to do some dirty work for you, I'll do that too. I'm now ready to join the club, where sharks eat sharks. And one day, while we are swimming around devouring the smaller fish—the water will become cloudy—with your blood—and that's when you will remember, that I wouldn't have joined, if it hadn't been for you.